Festivals of the *World*

SOUTH AFRICA

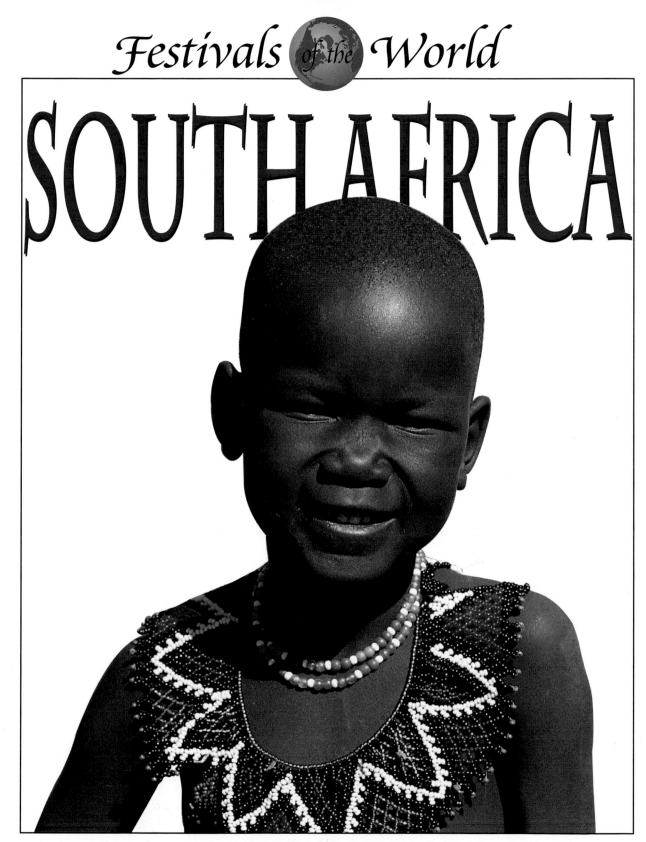

Gareth Stevens Publishing
MILWAUKEE

Written by
JAY HEALE

Edited by
TAN JIN HOCK

Designed by
HASNAH MOHD ESA

Picture research by
SUSAN JANE MANUEL

First published in North America in 1998 by
Gareth Stevens Publishing
1555 North RiverCenter Drive, Suite 201
Milwaukee, Wisconsin 53212 USA

For a free color catalog describing Gareth Stevens' list of high-quality books and multimedia programs, call
1-800-542-2595 (USA)
or 1-800-461-9120 (Canada).
Gareth Stevens Publishing's Fax: (414) 225-0377.
See our catalog, too, on the World Wide Web:
http://gsinc.com

© **TIMES EDITIONS PTE LTD 1998**
Originated and designed by
Times Books International
an imprint of Times Editions Pte Ltd
Times Centre, 1 New Industrial Road
Singapore 536196
E-mail: te@corp.tpl.com.sg
Printed in Singapore

Library of Congress Cataloging-in-Publication Data:
Heale, Jay.
South Africa / by Jay Heale.
p. cm.—(Festivals of the world)
Includes bibliographical references and index.
Summary: Describes how the culture of South Africa is reflected in its many festivals, including the Hermanus Whale Festival, Freedom Day, and the Grahamstown Festival.
ISBN 0-8368-2007-X (lib. bdg.)
1. Festivals—South Africa—Juvenile literature. 2. South Africa—Social life and customs—Juvenile literature. [1. Festivals—South Africa. 2. Holidays—South Africa. 3. South Africa—Social life and customs.]
I. Title. II. Series.
GT4889.S7H43 1998
394.26968—dc21   97-31587

1 2 3 4 5 6 7 8 9 02 01 00 99 98

CONTENTS

It's Festival Time . . .

South Africans just love a good occasion to celebrate. Happily, their Rainbow Nation of many races and religions offers plenty of opportunities to have an enjoyable time—Christmas and Easter, the Coon Carnival and Diwali, the Grahamstown Festival and whale welcoming parties, and many more! So, come along and join in the fun. It's festival time in South Africa . . .

WHERE'S SOUTH AFRICA?

Covering the southern tip of the African continent, South Africa has a countryside as mixed as its people. Around the southern coast are mild valleys where grapes, oranges, and apples grow. The central area is a semidesert called the **Karoo**. To the north are wide, high-level plains where farmers grow wheat, maize, and sunflowers. In the almost tropical northeast lies the Kruger National Park, one of the world's largest wildlife reserves.

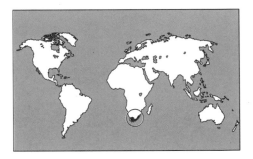

South Africans of all races are now working toward a common future together, a future based on trust and understanding.

Who are the South Africans?

Welcome to the land of the Rainbow Nation! Ever since the country's first free and fair elections in 1994 swept away the last vestiges of **apartheid**, South Africa has been proud to use Archbishop Desmond Tutu's description of the nation: "The rainbow people of God." Three-quarters of the population are black Africans. Their largest cultural groups are the Zulu and Xhosa. The rest are Europeans, Indians, Chinese, and brown-skinned people of mixed origin who are sometimes called "coloreds."

Opposite: The imposing Table Mountain carves out one of the world's most scenic natural settings for Cape Town.

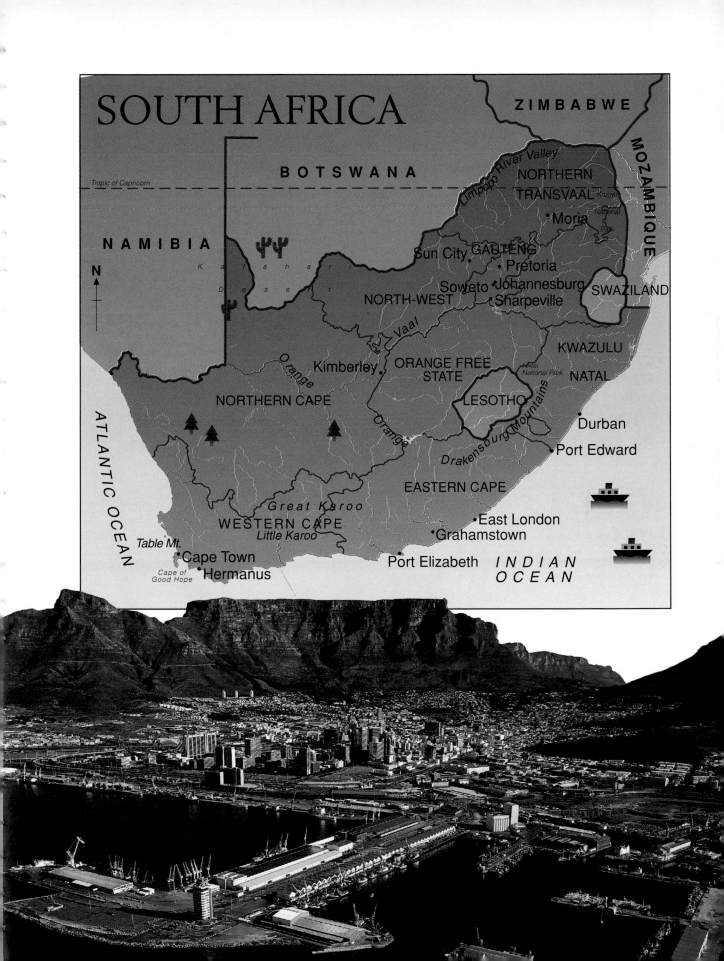

SOUTH AFRICA

ZIMBABWE

MOZAMBIQUE

BOTSWANA

Tropic of Capricorn

Limpopo River Valley

NORTHERN
TRANSVAAL

Krüger National Park

NAMIBIA

Kalahari Desert

• Moria

N

Sun City • GAUTENG
• Pretoria

Soweto • • Johannesburg
• Sharpeville

SWAZILAND

NORTH-WEST

Vaal

KWAZULU

NATAL

Orange

Kimberley •

ORANGE FREE
STATE

Natal National Park

NORTHERN CAPE

Orange

LESOTHO

Drakensburg Mountains

• Durban

• Port Edward

ATLANTIC OCEAN

Great Karoo

WESTERN CAPE
Little Karoo

EASTERN CAPE

Table Mt.
• Cape Town
Cape of Good Hope • Hermanus

Port Elizabeth

• East London
• Grahamstown

INDIAN OCEAN

WHEN'S THE CELEBRATION?

With a population including Christians, Muslims, Jews, and Hindus, there are far too many South African festivals to list them all. Here are some major ones, though.

SPRING

- ✪ **HERMANUS WHALE FESTIVAL**
- ✪ **DIWALI**
- ✪ **HERITAGE DAY**—A celebration of the art, music, and literature South Africans have inherited.

Come on! Join us as we jog around some of our festivals in the coming pages.

SUMMER

- ✪ **THE DAY OF RECONCILIATION**—Marks a new understanding between the different races of South Africa. It replaces the "Day of the Vow," which marked the victory of the Boers over the Zulus at the Battle of Blood River.
- ✪ **HANUKKAH**
- ✪ **CHRISTMAS**
- ✪ **NEW YEAR**

6

Phew! With all the fun and excitement in this book, it's hard to keep one's head!

AUTUMN

✪ **HUMAN RIGHTS DAY**— Commemorates the occasion in 1960 when police opened fire on a group of demonstrators in the township of Sharpeville near Johannesburg. They were protesting unjust apartheid laws. This day is a reminder to South Africans that human rights now form the basis of their constitution.

✪ **GOOD FRIDAY, EASTER DAY, AND FAMILY DAY**—About three million black African members of the Zion Christian Church make an annual Easter pilgrimage to Moria, in the northern part of the country. (Easter Monday is known as Family Day.)

✪ **PESACH (PASSOVER)**—To the Jews, a celebration of freedom.

✪ **FREEDOM DAY**—Celebrates the first democratic election for South Africa on April 27, 1994.

✪ **RAMADAN AND EID UL-FITR**—Important for the many Muslims in South Africa.

✪ **WORKERS' DAY**—A reminder that all people who work deserve a fair wage and decent working conditions.

✪ **SHEIKH YUSUF PILGRIMAGE**

WINTER

✪ **YOUTH DAY**—Honors the young people who died in the struggle against apartheid. Especially remembered are those killed by police in Soweto outside Johannesburg in June 1976 when they were protesting against their poor education. Special programs are put on in schools for Youth Day, often with sporting or cultural events.

✪ **GRAHAMSTOWN FESTIVAL**

✪ **NATIONAL WOMEN'S DAY**—Commemorates the march by about 20,000 members of the Federation of South African Women in Pretoria in 1956. It gives courage to women everywhere who suffer from discrimination.

7

NEW YEAR

The idea of celebrating the start of a new year is a very old one. The Roman god Janus was thought to have two faces: one for looking forward, the other for looking back. The first month of the year, January, is named after him. Everybody looks forward to a better year ahead.

The earliest Dutch settlers in South Africa sometimes celebrated the New Year for as long as two weeks. They said farewell to the Old Year by making bonfires, throwing fireballs, and ringing bells at midnight to scare away evil spirits. Then the New Year was greeted with feasts (including specially-baked, round, sweet biscuits) and sports contests, such as tug-o'-war and races on foot or horseback.

At New Year, the early Dutch immigrants would watch the weather carefully—the first week's weather was said to predict the weather for the whole year. These days, participants in the annual Coon Carnival in Cape Town are more likely to wish for bright sunshine to enjoy the festivities!

New Year's Day

Guess who is dropping by for dinner. A warthog decides to join a braai.

In South Africa, December marks the end of the school year. On December 31st, thousands of students wait for their examination results (known as "matric," short for matriculation) to find out whether they have qualified for university. Midnight beach parties take place if they have passed! Most families have a party to "see the new year in," perhaps with that South African favorite, a **braai** (br-EYE), or barbecue, with roasted meats and salads and plenty to drink. New Year's Day often includes watching **cricket** matches between such traditional provincial rivals as Western Cape and Gauteng.

Teenage girls in Natal welcome the New Year.

Get ready for the battle of the bands! There is hot competition to be judged the best. Groups with names like "Good Hope Entertainers" and "The Beach Boys" even have their own dance routines and specially-made costumes.

Tweede Nuwejaar

Slaves were brought to the southwestern part of South Africa around Cape Town (mostly from the East Indies and Malaya) as soon as the first Dutch settlement was established in the 1650s. By 1795, the slave population of the Cape was as high as 17,000. Although Britain abolished the slave trade in its colonies in 1807, South African slaves were not set free until December 1, 1834. Tradition has it that they then took a month's holiday—until January 1st.

In later years, they decided that one day's holiday (on New Year's Day) was simply not enough, so in the Cape (where most of the freed slaves lived) they instituted "Tweede Nuwejaar," or Second New Year's Day. The two-day holiday became the occasion for what is still called the "Coon Carnival," when descendants of the freed slaves parade through the streets with bands and singing.

Although January 2nd is no longer an official holiday, somehow that is forgotten in Cape Town!

10

Daar kom die Alabama!

One of the songs you are sure to hear from the Coons will be "Daar kom die Alabama," which means "Here comes the Alabama!" That song has quite a history. In 1863, the Yankees were fighting the Confederates in a civil war far from South Africa in a place called America! The *Alabama* was a Confederate ship that caught up with the Yankee vessel *Sea Bride* in full view of Cape Town. Everyone onshore was watching! The *Sea Bride* tried to sail away, but the *Alabama* had steam engines as well as sails and caught up easily. The Yankee ship and crew were taken prisoner, the *Alabama* sailed into Cape Town harbor, and a huge celebration went on for a long time. A song was written (in the Afrikaans language) for the occasion: "Here comes the *Alabama*! The *Alabama* is coming over the sea!"

During the Coon Carnival, children wear colorful costumes, take part in parades, and generally have a great time!

Think about this
South Africa now has two national anthems. One, *Die stem van Suid-Afrika* (The call of South Africa), was instituted by the old Afrikaner regime; the other, *Nkosi sikelel' iAfrika* (Lord bless Africa), is the anthem of the black African people, and it is used by other African countries as well. This is one clear indication how white people and black have agreed to come together.

11

GRAHAMSTOWN FESTIVAL

Grahamstown was once the second largest town in South Africa. One of the most fierce and desperate battles in local history took place here in 1819, when the townsfolk fought off an attack by 10,000 Xhosa warriors. Most people today connect the town with a very important date in South African history. In 1820, boatloads of British settlers arrived in the Cape, and Grahamstown became their main base. In their honor, the 1820 Settlers National Monument was built—a hilltop complex with conference halls and a theatre. Since 1974, this has been the focal point of a yearly arts festival that rivals the famous Edinburgh Arts Festival in Scotland.

This page: Contrasting modern and traditional cultural performances during the Grahamstown Festival.

Opposite: African crafts for sale at the Grahamstown Craft Market.

Left: Three happy painted faces— you will get to see many of these during the Grahamstown Festival! Many valuable awards are presented—to writers and to the young future stars of drama, fine art, and opera. It's nonstop culture, with quick meals in between. A not-to-be-missed occasion for the many people in South Africa who normally live far from live entertainment.

Below: An orchestra attracts a large and appreciative crowd.

Lots of activities!

The festival includes plays ranging from Shakespeare to slapstick comedy, music from opera to jazz, art exhibitions, a film festival, dance and ballet, lectures, and a special Children's Festival incorporating music, craftwork, drama, storytelling, and food. The best actors, singers, musicians, and dancers in South Africa all want to be part of the program.

Those visiting the Festival plan each day like a school timetable, buying tickets for five or six shows every day. They can watch artists in action, hear music from all over southern Africa, and watch theatrical performances in many languages.

A town alive

Hotel rooms in Grahamstown are all booked months before. So Rhodes University makes student accommodations available for visitors, and townsfolk rent out spare rooms at a handsome profit. The streets and car parks are filled with entertainers, food stalls, and souvenir sellers.

Several large areas are set aside for the ever-growing Craft Market, where you can buy T-shirts of your own design, candles, carpets, kites, pottery, stained glass, carved wood—all individually created by hand. Children in South Africa have made wire cars for years and played with them. Now they sell the cars to tourists, as well as windmills and candlesticks made of wire.

For 11 days of July each year, Grahamstown goes wild! Then, apart from its university, it goes back to sleep again.

Think about this

On the grounds of the 1820 Settlers National Monument building stand the four Freedom Stones. They commemorate the granting of democratic rights to all South Africans during the elections of April 1994, and they stand (as President Franklin D. Roosevelt of the United States defined in 1941) for the four important democratic freedoms:

Freedom of Speech
Freedom of Worship
Freedom from Fear
Freedom from Want

FESTIVALS OF LIGHT

T he coming of light from darkness is one of the most ancient signs of hope and goodness. The early inhabitants of Africa placed their rock paintings facing the sunrise, and many black African people built their homes so the rising sun could shine in through the doorway. Today, lights are used in most South African festivals, whether in the form of candles, electric lights, or fireworks.

Music is an important part of the Christmas tradition. Black South African musicians are renowned for their great sense of rhythm.

Christmas

Many South Africans are Christians, either in the accepted European style or a combination of Christianity and traditional African beliefs. Christians regard Jesus as "the light of the world," and at Christmastime they enjoy open-air carol services with everyone holding a lighted candle. Electric lights sparkle on Christmas trees and in the streets. The town of Somerset West, near Cape Town, has some of the most spectacular Christmas lights in the country. Families pile presents around the Christmas tree and open them either on Christmas Eve or Christmas morning.

Above and opposite: Christmas lights—some say they stand for the stars that shone above Bethlehem at the time of Jesus' birth.

16

Hanukkah

In Jewish homes, Hanukkah is the festival of light. It is a reminder of a time in Israel when the sacred Temple in Jerusalem returned to Jewish hands after a long period of foreign rule. The Jews searched for holy oil to relight the Temple lamp, but they could find only one small pot.

Yet, by some miracle, it kept burning for eight days. So, at Hanukkah time, Jews light one candle of the eight-branched *menorah* (meh-NOR-eh) candlestick for each day of the festival, while reciting special prayers.

Hanukkah is a happy time, with Jewish families giving presents and playing traditional games.

Think about this
Many South Africans arrange fireworks displays for November 5th. This custom has its origin deep in England's history. About 300 years ago, a man named Guy Fawkes tried to blow up the Parliament building in London. That means nothing to most South Africans though. They just enjoy fireworks!

Diwali

Most of South Africa's Hindus live in and around Durban on the eastern coast. For Hindus, Diwali is the most important festival of the year. Its main significance is to drive darkness from the mind and to bring light into the heart and home. Diwali means "a row of lamps," and no one is sure how it started! A traditional story from Indian folklore tells how Prince Rama and his wife Sita were banished from their home for 14 years. Sita was captured by the ten-headed demon Ravana, who took her away to his island. Rama rescued his wife with the help of Hanuman, the monkey god, and killed Ravana. The people of Rama's kingdom lit myriads of little clay lamps to guide him and Sita safely home. So, at Diwali time, *diva* (dee-wah) lamps twinkle a message of goodwill and unity, geometrical *rangoli* (ran-goo-lee) patterns are made on doorsteps or windows, and electric lights and garlands decorate the streets.

This page: Temples in Durban. Hinduism has many gods and goddesses, and their birthdays and marriage anniversaries are occasions for celebration in homes and temples. Hinduism really comes alive during these festivals!

WHALE-WATCHING IN HERMANUS

Words like *environment* and *ecology* usually make us think of endangered animals and plants. We don't often remember that there is a huge world inside our oceans that needs our attention and awareness as well. One of the largest problems (and the largest mammal, too!) concerns the whale. Some species are currently in danger of disappearing forever.

The most common species is the southern right whale. Whale hunters had once reduced its local population to as few as 100, but since it became protected in 1935, there are now well over 1,000. Twenty years ago, a movement was started to protect whales and dolphins.

Above: Great whales can still be seen from the shores of South Africa.

Left: A hand-colored woodcut of what whaling was like in the 1860s. South Africa once had whaling stations where slaughtered whales were cut up, and their blubber made into oil for soap, margarine, and candles.

The biggest of them all!

Whales comes in many sizes, big and small. The largest of all the whales, the blue whale, can grow up to 110 feet (33.6 meters) long and weigh more than 150 tons (136,000 kilograms). That's probably bigger than even the largest prehistoric dinosaur! The beluga whale, on the other hand, only averages about 15 feet (4.5 m).

Although they may look like fish, whales are warm-blooded mammals, just like humans. The whales breathe air through a blowhole on top of the head when they come to the water's surface. Their young are also born live, unlike fish, which are hatched from eggs.

Visitors from all over come to the town of Hermanus to search for whales that sometimes swim very close to shore.

21

All around the coast

Not all festivals in South Africa are old ones. Just as there is a new South Africa, so South Africans find reasons for celebrating in new ways. The newly-started Welcoming the Whales Festival encourages the growing desire for environmental awareness as well as linking whale-watching with having fun. Adults take part in related activities, such as sports, fun runs, and outdoor cooking competitions, while children draw pictures, dream up slogans, and write welcome messages for the whales. This happens in early June all along the southern coastal towns of the country. But there is one town that already has its own whale festival.

Spotting a whale is not easy! You have to be very patient just to catch a glimpse of these elusive creatures.

Want to play a game of beach cricket? Cricket is also very popular in countries such as Australia, England, and India.

Hermanus Whale Festival

Hermanus is a seaside town on the southwestern coast, built partly beside a wide lagoon ideal for yachting. It was named after a wandering scholar named Hermanus Pieters who first followed a path over the mountains and discovered an unspoiled bay. Fishermen and those who burned shells to make lime followed, and by 1868 the growing village opened its first school and church, named after St. Peter, the fisherman.

In September, the Hermanus Whale Festival is a way to greet the spring and the joy of living. It is also the time of year when the southern right whales come to sheltered waters to give birth to their calves. Hermanus employs a unique Whale Crier. Dressed in the style of the old English Town Crier, this man is equipped with a long horn (made of dried kelp, a type of seaweed) with which he announces a whale in sight. Different horn signals indicate in which area of water the whales have been spotted.

Visitors to the festival can take a guided Whale-Watching Walk along the cliff path and glimpse the whales close to shore. They can also enjoy the wild flowers and seaside birdlife. Most people, however, come for the 10 days of sports contests, shows and concerts, food, and fun.

Think about this
Is there a festival in *your* country that is dedicated to the environment or endangered animals?

Can't find the whales? Let Pieter Classen, the world's first Whale Crier, show you the right places.

WHALE CRIER HERMANUS

TODAY'S SIGHTINGS:
WINSOR HOTEL (2)
OLD HARBOUR (2)
ONDERSTEUN ASSEBLIEF
ONS
WALVIS MUSEUM
PROJEK
THANK YOU
DANKIE

SHEIKH YUSUF PILGRIMAGE

O n lonely sand dunes a good distance from Cape Town stands a shrine with white walls and a green domed roof. This shelters the grave of Sheikh Yusuf, the first great Muslim leader in South Africa. Legend relates that he showed his power even on the long voyage from the East Indies. When the ship's water supply ran out, the sheikh supposedly dipped his foot in the sea and buckets of fresh water were pulled up. Sent to the Cape in 1694 as a political prisoner, Sheikh Yusuf conducted religious services and encouraged missionary work among the slave community in and around Cape Town.

Left and opposite top: South Africa's Muslims are members of a religion that has hundreds of millions of believers around the world. Some five million Muslims live in the United States alone.

Sheikh Yusuf's tomb

The tomb of Sheikh Yusuf, called a ***kramat***
(KRAH-mart), is one of six special Muslim
tombs which, from tradition, are said to form a
"holy circle." An old teaching assured Muslims
that if they lived within this holy circle, they
were safe from all disasters, such as plague and
fire. Although only a few followers still believe
this, the kramat of Sheikh Yusuf is still regarded
as the most holy of them all. **Pilgrims** often
visit the shrine, perhaps bringing expensive silk
cloths to put on his tomb. Bottles of water from
the nearby river are sometimes left in the
shrine overnight in the belief that the water
will miraculously gain healing powers.

Right: Once a year, hundreds
of Muslims make pilgrimages
to South Africa's kramats.

THINGS FOR YOU TO DO

Toys made from wire have been popular with South African children for years. They are simple and inexpensive to make, yet great fun. You can even invent your own toys!

Wire cars and bicycles

Children in South Africa learn to make wire toys from an early age. Older children will teach the younger ones. This way, the skill is passed down. Wire cars are a favorite, but buses, bicycles, windmills, and candlesticks are popular, too. All that is needed is some metal wire, a pair of pliers, and lots of imagination. Perhaps you might even like to make one yourself!
Have fun!

Sing the South African anthem

The new joint national anthem of South Africa, "Nkosi sikelel' iAfrika" (Lord bless Africa), is familiar to many black Africans throughout the African continent. This famous song should be sung gently and smoothly.

Lord Bless Africa

Things to look for in your library

All About South Africa. (Struik, 1995 – revised edition).
Diwali. Chris Deshpande (A & C Black, 1994).
Guide to the Kramats of the Western Cape. (Cape Mazaar Society, 1996).
Nelson Mandela. Richard Killeen (Wayland, 1995).
South Africa. David Flint (Thomson Learning, 1996).
South Africa: A Journey of Discovery. (International Video Network, 1992).
We Call the Whales. Patricia Schonstein Pinnock (African Sun Press, 1993).
Whales: Giant Marine Mammals. Andreu Llamas (Gareth Stevens, 1996).
Whales and Dolphins. Éva Plagányi (New Holland 1994).

MAKE A KITE

Kite-flying is a favorite way for South African children to have fun when the wind blows up. Here are some instructions to make your own kite. Try using the paintbrush and your imagination to create some exciting designs for your kite!

You will need:
1. A plastic bag
2. Two lightweight garden canes
3. String
4. Tape
5. Paints
6. Paintbrush
7. Paint tray
8. Pencil
9. Glue
10. Scissors
11. Xacto knife

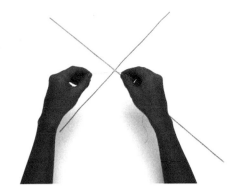

1 Cut a plastic bag into this kite shape.

2 Cut the cane to fit the shape of your kite. Cross the two lengths of cane into a "t" and tie at the center. These are the struts.

3 Tape the struts to the kite. Turn the kite over and put a piece of tape over the point where the struts cross.

4 Decorate your kite. Our kite is in the colors and design of the South African flag.

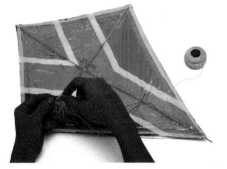

5 Cut a piece of string about twice the width of the kite. Tie one end securely around the intersection of the struts. This is the bridle. Thread the other end of the bridle through the bottom of the kite and tie. Finally, tie the flying line to the bridle, just above the center.

MAKE SOSATIES

These are some of the favorite items to grill over a fire in what South Africans call a braai (which means "roast"), but you call a barbecue. You can use almost any meat: lamb, beef, chicken, or pork. The secret lies in the marinade (sauce) in which you soak the meat overnight. So you really start the day before!

You will need:

1. ½ cup (80 grams) sweet chutney
2. ¼ cup (40 g) mayonnaise
3. ¼ cup (40 g) tomato sauce
4. A dash of Worcester sauce
5. 1 teaspoon mustard
6. ½ cup (120 ml) apple cider vinegar
7. ½ cup (120 ml) cooking oil
8. Small pieces of beef, pork, lamb, or chicken
9. A green pepper
10. A red pepper
11. Wooden skewers
12. Measuring cups
13. Measuring spoons
14. A knife
15. A whisk
16. A cutting board
17. A bowl

1 Whisk the first seven ingredients together in a bowl.

2 Have an adult help you chop the meat into small cubes. Leave them to soak in the sauce overnight—the longer the better! Then chop the green pepper and red pepper into bite-size pieces.

3 Prepare wooden skewers with a mixture of pieces of meat and pepper.

4 Ask your parents to help grill the sosaties. Delicious!

GLOSSARY

apartheid, 4 — A form of government in which people of different skin color are forced to live separately.

braai, 9 — A barbecue.

cricket, 9 — A game played with a ball and bat between two teams of 11 members each.

ecology, 20 — The relationship between all living organisms and their environment.

Karoo, 4 — A semidesert in central South Africa.

kramat, 25 — A Muslim holy shrine.

matric, 9 — Examination results, as they are known in South Africa.

menorah, 18 — Multi-branched candlestick used in the Jewish festival of Hanukkah.

pilgrim, 25 — A person who journeys a long distance to a sacred place as an act of devotion.

sosaties, 30 — Meat and vegetables cooked on a skewer (like a kebab).

INDEX

Picture credits
Andes Press Agency: 25 (top); Bes Stock: 28; Bruce Coleman: 5, 23; Christine Osborne Pictures: 26; David Houser: 2; Haga Library: 17; Hoa Qui: Title page, 10 (top); Hutchison: 4, 8, 9 (bottom), 11, 24; Images of Africa Photobank: 6, 9 (top), 13; Jan Butchofsky-Houser: 12 (bottom); Jason Lauré: 10 (bottom), 16 (bottom), 21 (top); Nic Bothma/i-Africa: 20 (top), 22 (bottom); Nik Wheeler: 25 (bottom); North Wind: 20 (bottom); South African Tourism Board: 3 (top), 12 (top), 14 (top), 15, 16 (top), 19 (both); Photobank: 3 (bottom); Still Pictures: 21 (bottom), 22 (top); Susanna Burton: 7 (top); Topham: 18; Travel Ink: 7 (bottom), 14 (bottom)